Kindergarten
Hooked on Learning®
Puzzles
and Mazes

Designed and illustrated by
Big Yellow Taxi, Inc.

The Rainy Day

Connect the dots from A to Z to help Pig Wig get out of the rain.

Stripes Are Nice

Use the key to color the umbrellas.

Key

1 =   2 =   3 =   4 =

Hooked on Learning *Puzzles and Mazes*

Get Dressed

Draw a path through the maze to get Pig Wig to her raincoat and hat. Hurry or she'll get wet!

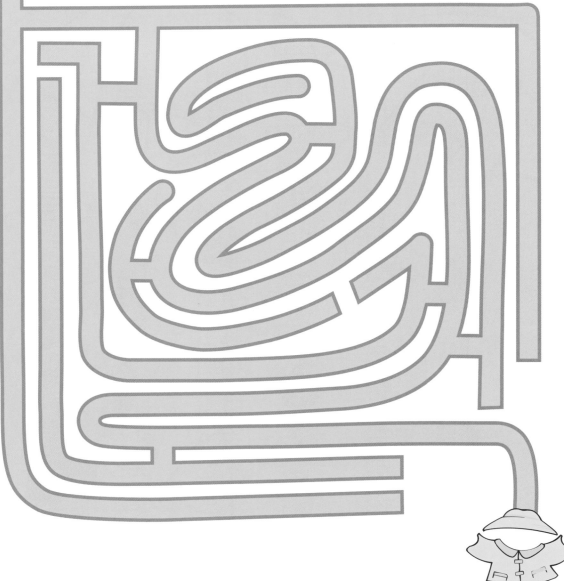

Puddle Fun

Who likes to stomp in puddles with Pig Wig?
Connect the dots from 1 to 40 to find out.

Hooked on Learning *Puzzles and Mazes*

Match Game

Circle the two boots that are exactly the same.

A Rainy Maze

Draw a path from raindrop to raindrop to help Hip-O get to Pig Wig's house.

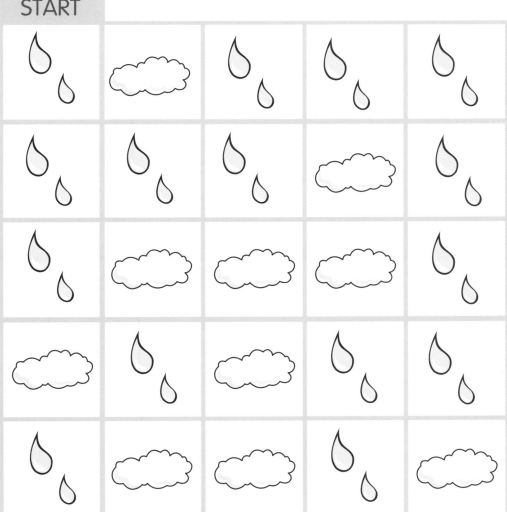

7

Puzzle Time

Finish Hip-O and Pig Wig's puzzle.
Circle the correct piece.

Hooked on Learning *Puzzles and Mazes*

Rainy-Day Play

Where will Hip-O and Pig Wig go on their pretend journey?
Say the name of each thing out loud.
Write the first letter of each thing's name on the line below it.

_____   _____   _____

_____   _____   _____   _____   _____

Hooked on Learning *Puzzles and Mazes*

Rainy-Day Music

The next time it rains, make some music!

Use the directions on the next page to make your own musical instruments.

Then tap, clap, or sing a song.

Before you know it, the sun will come out again!

Note to Parents
If you don't have the materials to make instruments, you can still have musical fun on a rainy day. Turn up the radio and have a dance party. Make up new dances with funny names, like "The Frog" or "The Slime."

Simple Shaker

You will need:

An empty jar with a lid
Dried beans, rice, or round cereal pieces

Fill the jar with beans or other small items. Close the lid tightly, then shake!

Quick Kazoo

You will need:

A paper-towel tube   Waxed paper
A rubber band

Punch a small hole near one end of the paper-towel tube. Cover that end with waxed paper and secure with a rubber band. Put your mouth by the open end and hum.

Rain Stick

You will need:

A paper-towel tube   Toothpicks   Dried beans
Rubber bands   Paper

Poke several toothpicks through the tube in different places. Cover one end of the tube with paper and secure with a rubber band. Put a big handful of dried beans in the tube. Cover the open end with paper and secure with a rubber band. Then gently move the tube back and forth to make the sound of rain as the beans travel over the toothpicks.

In for a Swim?

Circle the words that rhyme with **fin** in the puzzle.
Look across and down.

bin	pin	thin	tin	win

t	h	i	n	b	i
t	i	n	w	i	n
n	t	p	i	n	w

Hooked on Learning *Puzzles and Mazes*

That's A-maze-ing

Hip-O is ready to swim, too!
Draw a path through the maze.

Start

Finish

Sand Art

Hip-O and Pig Wig are building things in the sand.
What will they build? Is it a castle? A shark? A tower?
Use crayons to draw a picture of it!

Draw a Fish

Hip-O has found a fish!
Using a pencil and eraser, follow steps 1 to 4 to draw a fish.

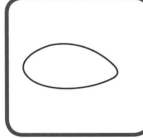

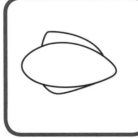

1. Draw the body shape.

2. Add top and bottom fins.

3. Add the tail fin.

4. Erase some lines, and add an eye.

Crab Chase

Pig Wig has found a crabby crab!
Draw a path through the maze to help Pig Wig get back to her umbrella.

Hooked on Learning *Puzzles and Mazes*

On the Beach

These pictures of Hip-O look the same, but they are different in 6 places.

Can you circle all of the things that are different?

17

Shell Search

Pig Wig is searching for seashells.
Can you find 10 shells hidden in this picture?

Hooked on Learning *Puzzles and Mazes*

Too Hot!

Pig Wig and Hip-O are thinking of something that will cool them off.
Say the name of each thing out loud.
Write the first letter of each thing's name on the line below it.

_____   _____   _____   _____

19

Hooked on Learning *Puzzles and Mazes*

Anywhere Games

You can play these games anywhere—on the beach, in a car, or while waiting in line at the supermarket.

You don't need any special items.

So what are you waiting for? It's game time!

Letter Search

Each player must find the letters of the alphabet in order. Look on signs, cars, buildings—even on clothing people are wearing. When you spot a letter, call it out! Whoever calls out the letters A to Z first is the winner.

Animal Alphabet

The object of this game is to think of the name of an animal that starts with each letter of the alphabet. The first player names an animal that begins with "a." Then the next player names an animal that begins with "b." If one player gets stuck, he can pass the letter to the next player. Keep going until one player gets to "z." Play this game with the names of people, food, or cartoon characters.

Count to 10

In this game, each player gets to shout out the name of something to count. In a car or a bus, a player might say, "Count 10 stop signs!" Then each player must look for 10 stop signs and count them out loud as he sees them. Keep naming things to count. On a beach, count 10 boogie boards, 10 blue bathing suits, 10 balls, 10 towels, or 10 seagulls.

Snow Good!

Hip-O and Pig Wig like playing in the snow.
Circle everything you see in this picture that begins
with the letter "s."

On Thin Ice

Use your finger to follow the tangled laces.
Which skates belong together?
Write your answers on the lines below.

1___   2___   3___   4___

Hooked on Learning *Puzzles and Mazes*

A Great Skate!

Draw a path through the letters to spell out "ice skate" so Hip-O can cross the pond and get some hot chocolate.

i	c	e	s	u
z	e	v	g	p
h	s	k	a	t
f	k	j	t	x
n	r	q	e	m

Finish

Hooked on Learning *Puzzles and Mazes*

A Frosty Friend

Help Pig Wig finish her snowman.
Draw a face and arms, then give the snowman a hat,
scarf, buttons, or whatever you want!

25

Down the Hill

How will Pig Wig get down the hill?
Connect the dots from 1 to 30 to find out.

Can you circle the penguin that is different?

Let It Snow

Can you find these three pictures in a row?
Look up, down, and across.
Circle the three when you find them.

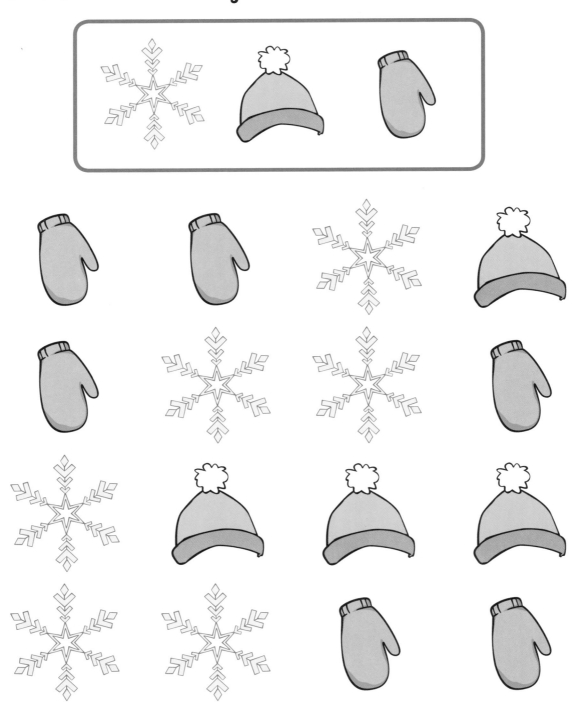

Let's Pretend

Hip-O and Pig Wig want to pretend they are somewhere with a lot of animals.
Say the name of each thing out loud.
Write the first letter of each thing's name on the line below it.

_____   _____   _____   _____   _____

29

Silly Snowman

This is a game for two players.

You will need:

A die

A pencil or crayon

How to play:

1. The first player rolls the die. He writes the number on the die next to the first word on the list on the next page. Then he draws that many eyes on his snowman.

2. Players take turns rolling the die for each part of the snowman.

3. Continue until the lists are complete.

Note to Parents
You may photocopy the blank snowmen on the next page so that you can play the "Silly Snowman" game again and again. If you play with your child, use your finished snowmen to practice basic math skills. Compare the number of eyes, noses, and so on. Ask questions such as "Does your snowman have more eyes than mine?" "Do they have the same amount?" "How many more arms does my snowman have?"

eyes _____

noses _____

arms _____

hats _____

buttons _____

eyes _____

noses _____

arms _____

hats _____

buttons _____

Hooked on Learning *Puzzles and Mazes*

Animals on the Farm

What animals will Pig Wig and Hip-O see on the farm?
Circle all the farm animals you see.

Rhyme Time

Look at the pictures in each row.
Say their names out loud.
Circle the thing whose name rhymes with the name
of the animal on the left.

hen

pig

ox

cat

33

The Chicken Coop

Pig Wig is feeding the chickens.
Using a pencil and eraser, follow steps 1 to 4 to
draw a chicken.

1. Draw shapes for the head and body.

2. Draw wings and a tail.

3. Draw feet.

4. Draw eyes, a beak, and a comb.

Hide and Seek

I did it!

Where is Hip-O hiding?
Connect the dots from 1 to 25 to find out.

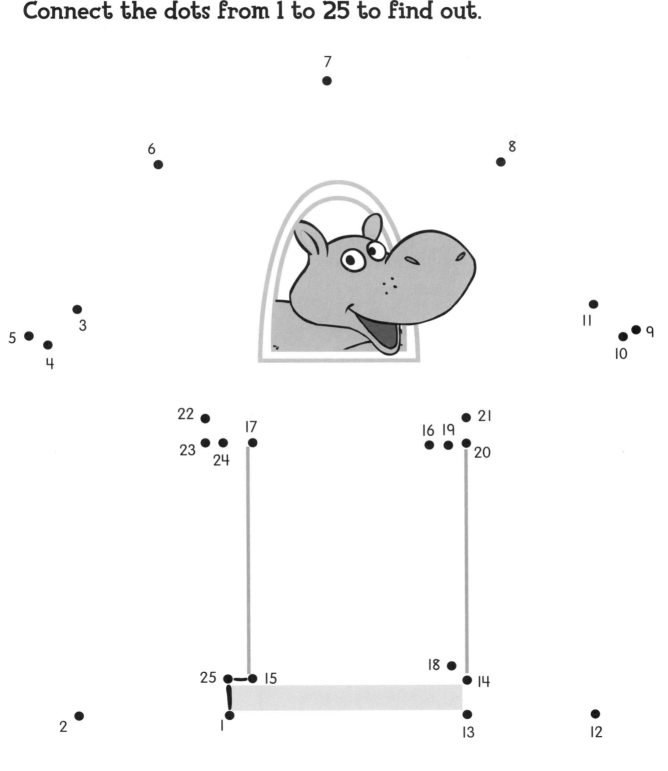

Hooked on Learning *Puzzles and Mazes*

Tractor Time

Draw a path through the maze to help Pig Wig find her way out of the cornfield.

Carrots and Corn

Draw a path through the carrots and corn to get from start to finish.

START

FINISH

Yummy Shapes

How many of each shape can you find on the table?
Write your answers on the lines.

◯ _____   △ _____

Hooked on Learning *Puzzles and Mazes*

Time to Eat!

Pig Wig and Hip-O are hungry. What will they eat?
Say the name of each thing out loud.
Write the first letter of each thing's name on the line
below it.

_____   _____   _____   _____   _____

Hooked on Learning *Puzzles and Mazes*

Stop to Shop

Pig Wig and Hip-O are shopping for food.
Draw a path through the maze to see who will get
to the cash register.

Food Hunt

Circle the food words hidden in the puzzle.
Look across and down.

apples bread cheese eggs

grapes milk juice

c	h	e	e	s	e
a	p	p	l	e	s
e	b	r	e	a	d
g	m	i	l	k	a
g	r	a	p	e	s
s	j	u	i	c	e

Hooked on Learning *Puzzles and Mazes*

Pizza Party

Pig Wig made a pizza.
Circle the picture that is **different** in each row.

42

Yum Yum!

Use the Key to color the picture.

Key

1 = 　　　　2 = 　　　　3 =

43

Pasta Tangle

Pig Wig and Hip-O like pasta, too.
Which bowl of pasta belongs to each friend?
Use your finger to follow the tangled pasta.
Write your answers on the lines below.

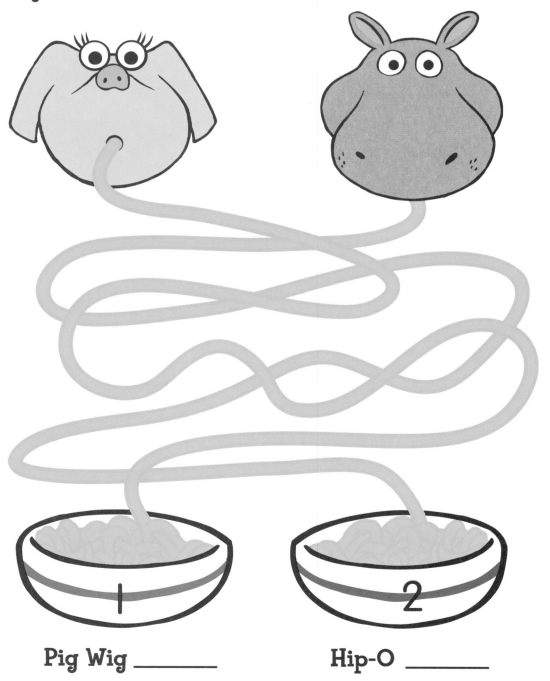

Pig Wig _____   Hip-O _____

A Pretty Plate

Pig Wig loves pizza.
What is your favorite food?
Draw your favorite thing to eat on the plate.

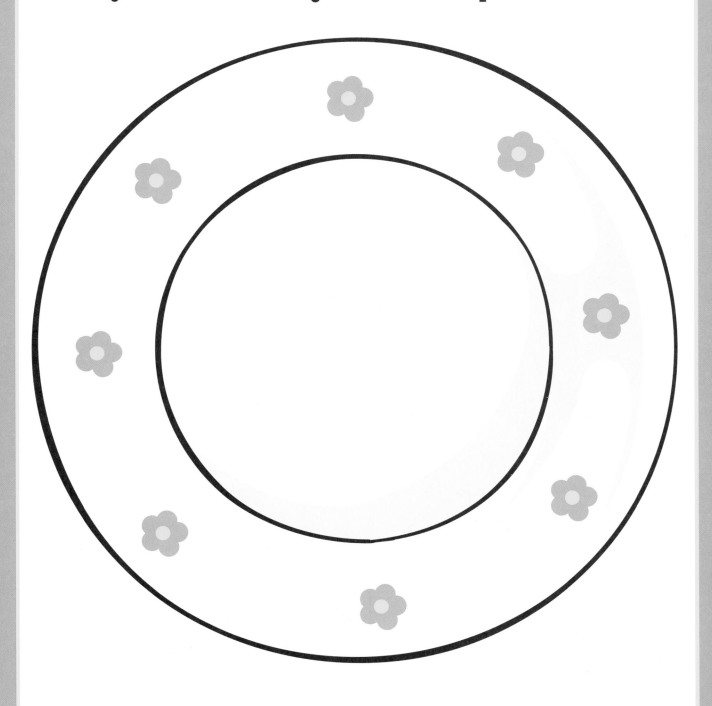

Hooked on Learning *Puzzles and Mazes*

What Comes Next?

Circle the picture that comes next in each pattern.

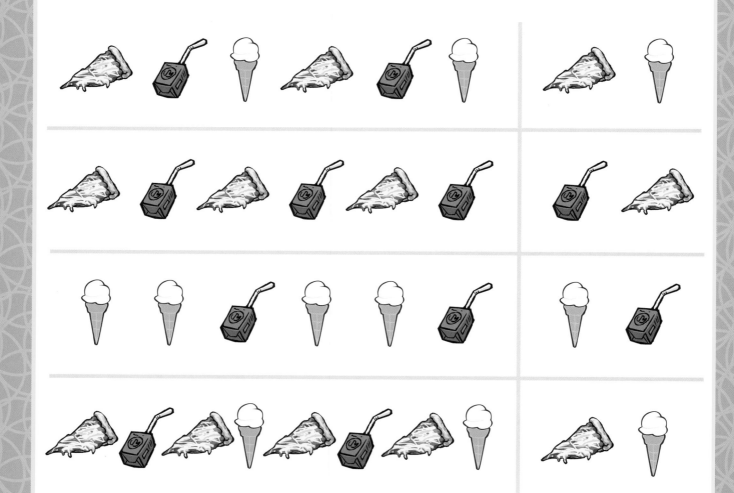

Holding Court

Who will Pig Wig and Hip-O pretend to meet now?
Say the name of each thing out loud.
Write the first letter of each thing's name on the line below it.

___ ___ ___ ___ ___

Hooked on Learning *Puzzles and Mazes*

Lost in the Castle

Pig Wig and Hip-O want to see the queen of the castle. Draw a path through the castle to help them find the queen.

The Perfect Plan

Use the pictures to help you read the story.

Once upon a time there was a . She lived

in a . The had a beautiful .

A lived near the . The liked .

He flew to the and took the .

The was sad. She called on and for

help. The asked them to go to the and get

back the .

 and  had a plan.

They knew how to get the back.

 packed a .

said, "Let's go!"

And that is just what they did!

Hooked on Learning *Puzzles and Mazes*

Colors in the Crown

What color is each gem?
Use the picture clues and the word box to fill
in the puzzle.

blue = ☐   yellow = ☐   orange = ☐
green = ☐   red = ☐

Across:

1.

5.

Down:

2.

3.

4.

The Dragon's Den

I did it!

Draw a path through the triangle-shaped jewels
to help Pig Wig and Hip-O get to the dragon's den.

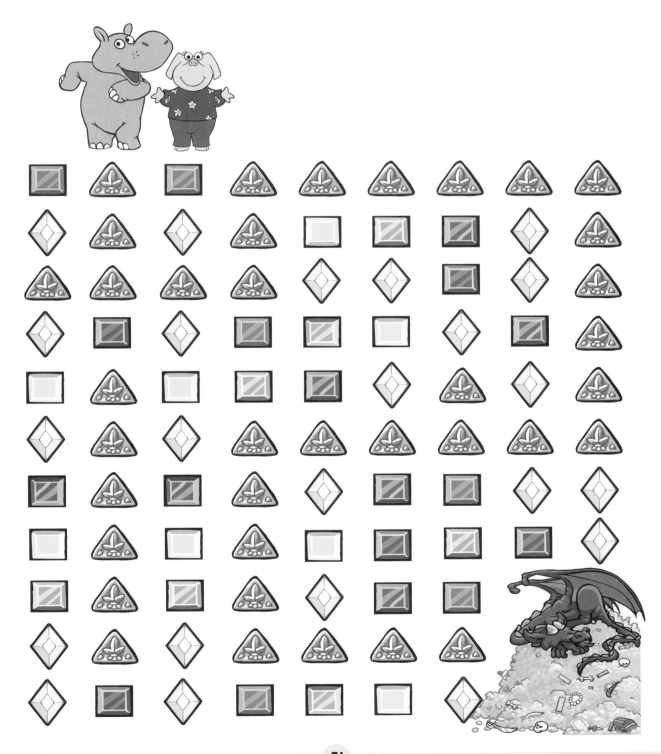

51

Hooked on Learning *Puzzles and Mazes*

Hidden Treasures

Can you find 11 crowns hidden in this picture?

A Fair Trade

Pig Wig and Hip-O want to make a trade with the dragon to get the crown.
Connect the dots from 1 to 20
to see what they brought to trade.

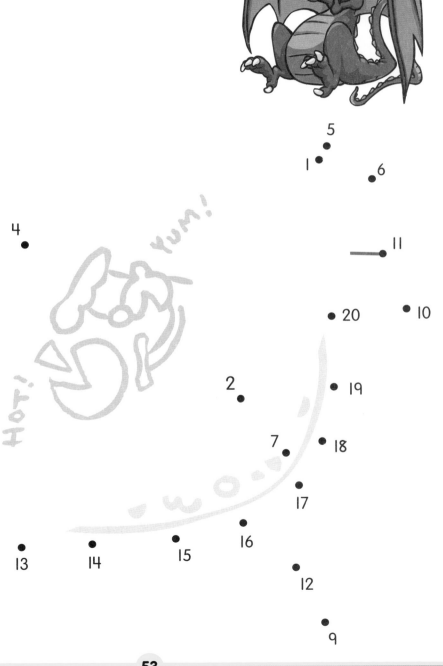

53

Color the Crown

The queen's crown is safe!
Use the Key to color the jewels in the crown.

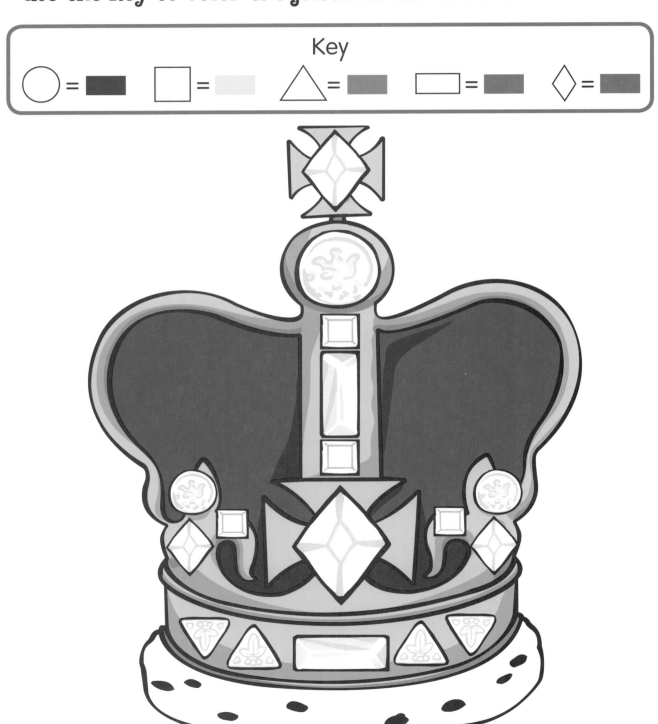

Different Dragons

These two dragons look the same, but they are different in 6 places.

Can you circle all of the things that are different?

55

Play Pretend

Hip-O and Pig Wig have fun playing pretend.

You can play pretend, too.

Write the names of the places in the box on index cards.

Place the cards face down. Pick a card.

Then pretend you are in that place.

What happens on your pretend adventure?

Draw a picture of it on the next page.

> **in the rain**
>
> **in the snow**
>
> **in a castle**
>
> **on the beach**
>
> **on a farm**
>
> **in a restaurant**

Note to Parents
You can make cards with additional places, such as the moon, a mountain, a big city, and so on. Take the activity further by writing a story with your child about his pretend adventure.

Hello, Sun!

Can you find these three pictures in a row?
Look up, down, and across.
Circle the three when you find them.

To the Park!

Draw a letter "p" path to get Pig Wig and Hip-O to the park.

p   a   o   b   e   h

p   m   p   p   p   k

p   p   p   n   p   u

v   x   s   r   p   t

z   b   a   h   p   p

n   c   y   d   c   p

Hooked on Learning *Puzzles and Mazes*

My Shadow

Draw a line from each picture of Pig Wig to the matching shadow.

Hat Hunt

Look at the hats on the page.
Circle the ones you have seen in this book.
Go back and look if you have to!

Hooked on Learning *Puzzles and Mazes*

Answer Key

PAGE 2

PAGE 3

PAGE 4

PAGE 5
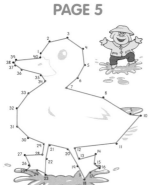

PAGE 6

PAGE 7

PAGE 8

PAGE 9
the beach

PAGE 12

t	h	i	n	b	i
t	i	n	w	i	n
n	t	p	i	n	w

PAGE 13

PAGE 16
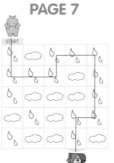

PAGE 17
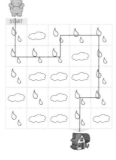

PAGE 18

PAGE 19
snow

PAGE 22
sun, sled, snowman
scarf, sticks, shovel

PAGE 23
1-c; 2-d;
3-a; 4-b

PAGE 24

PAGE 26

PAGE 27
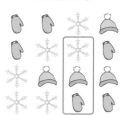

PAGE 28

PAGE 29
a farm

PAGE 32
cow, chicken, horse,
pig, sheep, goat

PAGE 33
hen/pen; pig/wig;
ox/box; cat/hat

PAGE 35
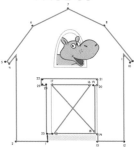

PAGE 36

PAGE 37
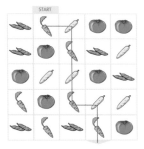

PAGE 38
14 circles, 5 triangles

PAGE 39
pizza

PAGE 40
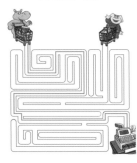

PAGE 41

PAGE 42

PAGE 43

PAGE 44
Pig Wig: 1
Hip-O: 2

PAGE 46
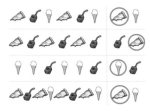

PAGE 47
queen

PAGE 48

PAGE 50
Across:
  1. orange
  5. yellow
Down:
  2. red
  3. green
  4. blue

PAGE 51
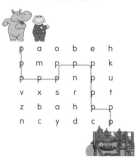

PAGE 52
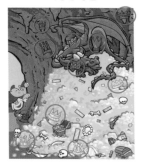

PAGE 53

PAGE 54

PAGE 55

PAGE 58

PAGE 59
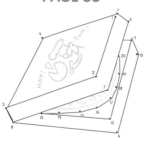

PAGE 60

PAGE 61

Hooked on Learning *Puzzles and Mazes*

I did it!

Congratulations!

_____

- - - - - - - - - - - - - - - - - - - -

_____

has successfully completed this workbook.

I did it!

Hooked on Learning®

Puzzles and Mazes

My Shadow
Hat Hunt

Hello,
Sun!
To the
Park!

Color
the Crown
Different
Dragons

Hidden
Treasures
A Fair
Trade

Colors
in the
Crown
The
Dragon's
Den

Lost in
the Castle
The Perfect
Plan

What
Comes Next?
Holding
Court

Pasta
Tangle
A Pretty
Plate

Pizza
Party
Yum
Yum!

Stop
to Shop
Food
Hunt

Yummy
Shapes
Time
to Eat!

Tractor
Time
Carrots
and Corn

The
Chicken
Coop
Hide and
Seek

Animals
on the Farm
Rhyme Time

Progress Poster

Start Here!

Let It Snow

Let's Pretend

Down the Hill

A Pile of Penguins

A Great Skate!

A Frosty Friend

Snow Good!

On Thin Ice

Shell Search

Too Hot!

Crab Chase

On the Beach

Sand Art

Draw a Fish

In for a Swim?

That's A-maze-ing

Puzzle Time

Rainy-Day Play

Match Game

A Rainy Maze

Get Dressed

Puddle Fun

The Rainy Day

Stripes Are Nice

HOOKED ON LEARNING

My name is